STEP INTO NATURE

Around a Tree

Written by Michael Chinery
Illustrated by John Gosler

GRANADA

Published by Granada Publishing 1984
Granada Publishing Limited
8 Grafton Street, London W1X 3LA

Copyright © Templar Publishing Ltd 1984
Illustrations copyright © Templar Publishing Ltd 1984

British Library Cataloguing in Publication Data
Chinery, Michael
  Around a tree.– (Step into nature; 7)
  1. Forest flora – Great Britain –
    Juvenile literature
  2. Forest fauna – Great Britain –
    Juvenile literature
  I. Title   II. Series
  574.941   QH138.A1

  ISBN 0-246-12178-5

Series devised by Richard Carlisle
Edited by Mandy Wood
Designed by Mick McCarthy
Printed in Italy

Contents

No matter where you live, you are surrounded by nature.
In the towns, even in the cities, you will find birds and animals,
flowers and trees, bugs and grubs to watch and wonder about.
STEP INTO NATURE is about all these things – the everyday
creatures as well as the elusive. It's packed with nature projects
to do, nature diaries to keep and clues and signs for the
nature detective to read. It will teach you how to look at the
world of nature around you, how to understand its working and
how to conserve it for others.

This is a tree!

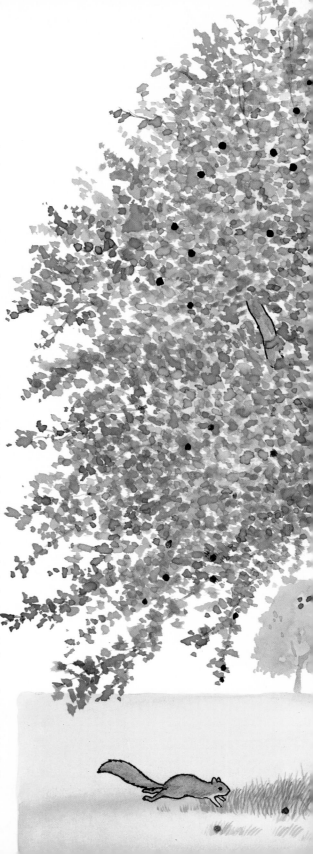

The largest living things growing on the earth are trees. The huge redwoods that grow in California, for example, reach heights of more than 100 metres. The Wellingtonia, which grows in the same area, is not quite as tall but its trunk is much thicker than the redwood trunk. One famous specimen, nick-named General Sherman, measures 24 metres around its trunk and stands 83 metres high. What's more, it's estimated to weigh 2030 tonnes!

Of course, most trees are much smaller than this, but they all have one thing in common – a large woody stem called the trunk. This is what distinguishes trees from all other plants. In most respects, they are just like the smaller plants that you see around you – except that they live a lot longer. They all have roots and leaves and they all produce seeds. Most trees also have flowers – which often look very like those from smaller plants – and these flowers also produce fruits. Pine trees and their relatives, known as conifers, are the exceptions – they have no flowers and produce their seeds in woody cones instead.

Many trees lose all of their leaves in the autumn and replace them with fresh ones in the spring. These are called deciduous trees. Those which keep their leaves throughout the winter are called evergreens and are found mainly in colder areas. Evergreen leaves do not live for ever, though. The tree simply replaces just a few leaves at a time.

The tree in the big picture is a plane tree. You can recognise it quite easily by its flaky bark. The plane is often planted in town parks and streets because it doesn't seem to mind the smoke and traffic fumes. You can find out more about the plane tree on page 22.

Inside the trunk!

Inside every tree trunk there is wood. But this wood is not the same all the way through. Beneath the bark, the trunk carries water to the leaves through thousands of tough-walled tubes which form the sapwood. New rings of these tubes are added each year (see page 37). The oldest tubes, in the centre, are gradually crushed to form the stronger heartwood.

Bark protects the trunk

Heartwood carries no water and is quite dead, although very strong

Sapwood carries water up to the leaves

New growth

In the past woodland trees such as ash and hazel were periodically cut to the ground and then allowed to regrow. The new shoots which sprang up after the treatment, called coppicing, provided long thin poles and had many uses. Hedgerow trees were usually cut higher up, so that cattle could not nibble the new shoots. This system is called pollarding. Look for coppiced and pollarded trees in the countryside.

A pollarded tree

A coppiced tree

Animal acrobats

Trees provide not only food and shelter, but also spacious playgrounds for the acrobatic squirrel. The commonest squirrel in Britain is the grey but, although it is seen much more often than the red, it is not a native animal. In fact, it was brought to England from North America late in the 19th century and has since spread to most parts of the country. Look for it in woods, parks and gardens – for wherever there are trees there will probably be grey squirrels. Watch it bound over the ground and scamper up and down the tree trunks. It spends quite a lot of time on the ground in autumn and winter, but stays mainly in the trees, gambolling among the branches, during the summer. Here it performs the most amazing tricks – running along slender branches like an expert tight-rope walker and making huge leaps through the air to reach neighbouring trees. Its sharp claws give it a good grip on the bark, while its long fluffy tail acts as a rudder for steering and balance.

The grey squirrel is a delightful animal to watch, but unfortunately it is a serious pest and does a lot of damage in the forest. Its favourite foods in spring and summer are buds and bark, and it often kills the tops of trees by stripping all the bark from them. It also eats nuts, fungi, insects and even birds' eggs. Look for hazel shells split neatly in half to show you where the squirrel has been feeding. You might also see it burying acorns and other nuts in autumn.

The squirrel builds its nest high in the trees. It is called a drey. You can see a baby peering out of the drey in the big picture. Apart from raising their babies there, squirrels also sleep in their dreys during the winter, but they do not hibernate like some other animals. You can see them searching for buried nuts all through the cold weather.

nature detective

Squirrel look-alikes

The two animals in this panel may look like the grey squirrel but they are not nearly so common. Both are nocturnal and you are more likely to see them in a zoo rather than in the wild.

The **flying squirrel** *(below)* lives in Finland and Russia. It does not really fly, but glides from tree to tree using the broad flaps of skin which it stretches out on each side of its body. It lives in birch forests and feeds mainly on buds and seeds.

The **glis-glis** or fat dormouse *(left)* is rare in Britain but common elsewhere in Europe. It likes tall trees. Notice its pink ears.

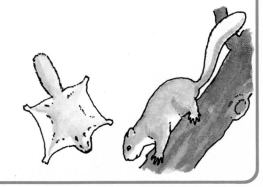

The life of a leaf

Leaves are a tree's food factories. They make sugars and other foods from water and minerals taken from the soil, and from carbon dioxide gas taken from the air. This food-making process is very complicated and is called *photosynthesis*. The green colouring matter in the leaves, called chlorophyll, plays an important part in the process. And so does sunlight, for it supplies the energy needed to make the food. In fact, photosynthesis actually means "making by light". The leaves give off oxygen gas during this complicated process, and lots of water vapour escapes from the tiny breathing pores on the leaves. There are thousands of these pores on the underside of each leaf, but you need a powerful microscope to see them. You can see the water they produce, though, by following the

1 The horse chestnut tree stands bare in winter (left). But the twigs are covered with large sticky buds, which have the next spring's leaves safely tucked up inside them. Notice the large horseshoe-shaped scars on the twigs. These show where the old leaves were once attached and give the tree its name. Groups of rings on the twigs show where the sticky bud scales were once attached.

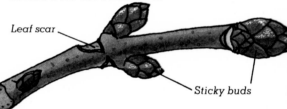

Leaf scar

Sticky buds

3 The new leaves, composed of several leaflets, soon reach full size. The new shoots become woody, and fresh buds appear on them – always at the base of the leaf stalk, never at the base of the leaflets themselves.

4 Towards autumn, the tree takes back all the goodness from its leaves and prepares for leaf-fall. The leaves change colour before falling and the trees take on their beautiful autumn colours of gold and brown.

experiment in the panel on the right.

Individual leaves do not live for very long. Deciduous trees, like the horse chestnut below, drop all their leaves in the autumn and the tree stands bare all through the winter. Evergreen trees, on the other hand, keep their leaves all year round. Their leaves are much tougher than deciduous leaves, as you will see if you look at holly leaves and pine needles, and they are not easily damaged by the winter winds. Thick waxy coats also ensure that they do not lose too much moisture – which is very important in the winter when the tree cannot absorb water from the frozen soil. Evergreen leaves do not live forever though. The tree drops and replaces some each year.

Collect some leaves from different types of tree. You'll probably find that although some leaves have completely smooth edges, most are toothed and some are deeply notched. You might find that others are completely divided into a number of leaflets, like those shown here. Leaves like this are called compound leaves.

2 The buds open in spring and the new leaves gradually expand. Soon the tree is clothed in rich green leaves (below). Soft new shoots grow from some buds and harden into new twigs. Other buds produce flower clusters.

Water from leaves

Try this simple experiment to prove that leaves give off water vapour. Tie a polythene bag around a leafy twig as shown below and leave it for a few hours. You will soon see lots of water droplets forming on the inside of the bag. You can use a twig in a jar of water or one still on the tree. Try the same experiment with another twig of the same kind, but this time smear the undersides of the leaves with grease. Do you get much water this time? Where are the breathing pores that give off the water vapour? Try the experiment again, without the grease, in a dark cupboard. How much water do you get this time? The leaves don't make food in the dark, so the breathing pores shut down to save water. Why do you think leaves wilt if you cut twigs and don't put them in water?

The nimble nuthatch

The sprightly little nuthatch, which you can see on the right, spends nearly all its life exploring tree trunks. Look for it on deciduous trees in woods, parks and large gardens. You will probably hear its loud bell-like call of *chewit-chewit* long before you see the bird itself. But if you're patient you may catch sight of it performing its amusing antics – hopping and leaping around the trunk, using its long claws to take a firm grip on the bark. Unlike the woodpeckers and other tree-climbing birds, the nuthatch can scamper up and down trees with equal ease and is quite happy to come down a trunk head-first, just as it's doing in the picture.

For much of the year the nuthatch feeds on insects and spiders, which it plucks from the bark with its long, slender beak. But during the autumn and winter the bird's main foods are nuts and seeds. Hazel nuts are its favourites. It picks them up with its beak and wedges them into bark crevices, usually fairly near the ground. Then, using all the power in its tiny body, the nuthatch hammers away at them with its beak, (as you can see in the small picture). Eventually, the nut will break open to reveal the juicy kernel, and the bird can at last get at its meal. Look for empty shells wedged in tree bark in the autumn. Unlike the woodpecker, the nuthatch has not learned to remove the shell and use the crevice again. Instead, it must search for a new crevice for each nut. So if you find a pile of shells with jagged holes in them, you can be fairly sure that you have found a woodpecker's dining room rather than one belonging to a nuthatch: look for the narrow, slit-like beak marks on the shells. The nuthatch leaves broader marks, like tiny half-moons, where it hammers the shells.

nature watch

Spot the treecreeper

At some 12 cms long, the treecreeper is a little smaller than the nuthatch. It spends nearly all its time creeping about tree trunks, where its mottled brown back makes it very difficult to see. Even if you do spot it, you might at first mistake it for a sparrow, but its long curved beak and white belly clearly identify it. Treecreepers feed entirely on insects and spiders, which they find in the bark crevices. You can find these birds on coniferous trees as well as on the broad-leaved deciduous kinds. Watch them move jerkily up the trunks as they search for food, propping themselves up with their very stiff tail feathers. They can also be seen exploring the undersides of larger branches, but they cannot come down trunks like the nuthatch. When they reach the top, they always fly down and start to climb all over again. They nest in deep crevices or behind loose bark.

Eyes that lie

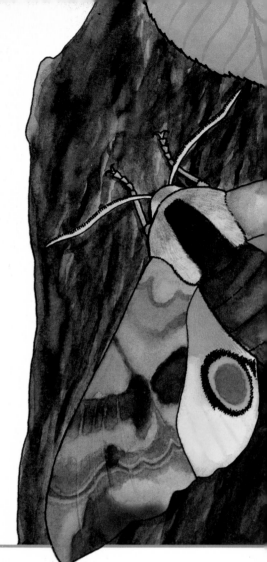

The moth in this picture is certainly well named. It is called the eyed hawkmoth. But the colourful "eyes" on its hind wings are not real: they are just a part of its wing pattern and they are there to deceive its enemies – the birds.

The eyed hawkmoth is one of many moths that rest on tree trunks during the day. If you look at the life-size moth in the circle you can see how different it looks when at rest and how, despite its large size, it becomes much more difficult to spot on the tree trunks when its wings are closed. However, if the eyed hawkmoth is disturbed, it will raise its front wings to reveal the big eye-spots and also sway to and fro. Its enemies are fooled into thinking that the eyes belong to a much bigger animal and this is enough to frighten most of them away. Having succeeded in its trickery, the hawkmoth closes its wings and continues with its rest.

Several other moths bluff their way out of trouble like this, but most avoid their enemies by being cleverly camouflaged. You can see some of these devious disguises in the panel below.

nature detective

Tree trunk moths

Examine tree trunks for resting moths in the daytime. Early morning is best because, despite their camouflage, some of them will be found by birds during the day.

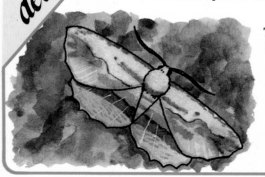

The **waved umber moth** (left) sits with its brown striped wings pressed flat against the bark. It is difficult to spot even when you are very close by. It flies in April and May.

The **swallow prominent moth** (above) rests with its wings folded along the sides of its body which makes it look just like a piece of bark or a broken twig. Look for it in spring and summer.

Drunken moths!

Most moths come out to fly at night, so in order to study them various different traps are used. One interesting method is to go "sugaring". Most moths are very fond of sweet things and you can attract quite a lot by using a mixture of treacle and beer. Mix two measures of treacle for each measure of beer. A crushed pear-drop added to the mixture will help. Then paint streaks of the mixture on tree trunks at sunset and go back every half-hour to see what insects have arrived. See how the moths stick their long tongues out to suck up the mixture. They get quite drunk! Warm summer nights are best, and solitary trees are better than those in woods.

The **pale tussock moth** (left) also matches lichen-covered bark beautifully. This is a female. The male is more slender and has feathery antennae. It flies in May and June.

The **peach blossom moth** (above) looks bright enough here, but is surprisingly hard to see on a tree trunk. It flies in June.

This **peppered moth** (right) matches lichen-covered bark very well. You might even see a black form of this moth which occurs mainly in urban areas and blends with the smoke-blackened tree trunks. The moth flies from May to July.

The sturdy oak

The tree on the right is known as the English oak, although it grows in most other parts of Europe as well. It is well-known for providing the sturdy timbers used in old ships and many famous buildings, for the oak's heartwood (see page 5) is extremely strong and resistant to decay.

The English oak is a deciduous tree which likes rich, moist soils. Look for it in old parkland as well as in woods. Notice its huge twisted branches which begin quite low down on the trunk. You can see them easily in the winter when the leaves have fallen and the branches are bare, like the tree in the drawing below.

See if you can find an oak tree growing locally and watch it throughout the year. Look for the winter buds, clustered tightly around the tips of the shoots. These buds open in late spring to reveal the tree's pale green leaves which soon expand to their full size. The flowers appear at about the same time. The male ones grow in slender catkins which scatter pollen in the breeze. But the female flowers, which produce the fruits of the tree (called acorns), are much more difficult to see. They are like tiny brown pin-heads which appear at the tips of the new shoots. Later in the year the acorns themselves appear. They have long stalks and turn brown and woody as they ripen in autumn. They are eaten by many different creatures, such as the fallow deer which you can see in the picture. But enough survive each year to produce new oak trees. Try to find out the ages of some of your local oaks (see page 37).

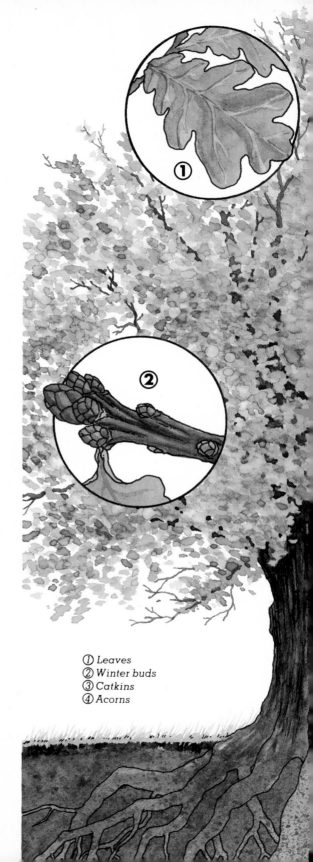

① Leaves
② Winter buds
③ Catkins
④ Acorns

Which oak is which?

How many different kinds of oak tree can you find? Look for them in parks and gardens as well as in the woods. Some are deciduous and some are evergreen, but all bear their acorns in little cups. Many foreign oaks are now grown in Britain.

The **Turkey oak** *(left)* is a deciduous tree from southern Europe. Its leaves are deeply divided and its acorn cups are always "furry". You can recognise the tree in winter because its buds are "furry" as well!

The **holm oak** *(right)* is an evergreen tree from southern Europe. The dark, shiny leaves are hairy underneath and somewhat spiny on young trees. The bark is very dark and cracks into small squares. Holm oak is commonly planted in seaside parks and gardens.

The **sessile oak** *(left)*, also known as the durmast oak, is much like the English oak but it has stalked leaves and stalkless acorns. Its branches tend to be straighter than in the English oak. It grows mainly in the upland areas of northern and western Britain.

③

④

15

Which bird is which?

Trees give food and shelter to many different kinds of birds and also provide an ideal place for them to make their nests – sometimes woven among the branches, sometimes tucked away in a hole. Use your binoculars to see how many different kinds of birds you can find in the trees.

Draw up a chart of trees and birds in your *Nature Diary*. With the bird names along the top and the tree names down the side, you can easily tick off which birds you find in which trees. Do some birds like certain trees better than others? Are any trees disliked by the birds?

If the birds are feeding, try to discover what they are eating. You will see some eating fruits and seeds while others search for insects. Do you see any actually eating leaves? On this page you can see some of the slightly less common birds of the trees. Keep a look out for them in the countryside.

The **hawfinch** is one of the largest finches. Its huge beak, which is yellow in winter, is used to crack open hard nuts and seeds – it can even crack cherry stones. Look for the hawfinch in deciduous woods, orchards and parks where there are plenty of trees. It is a shy bird and likes to stay high in the branches.

The **siskin** is a small finch. You can recognise the male by his black chin and crown. The streaky female is less easy to identify, but she always has yellow at the base of her tail. Siskins breed mainly in coniferous woods, but you will see them in other trees in the winter. Like all finches, they eat seeds.

The **chiff-chaff** is an insect-eater belonging to the warbler family. It likes tall trees and you will probably hear it long before you see it . It gets its name because it calls *chiff-chaff, chiff-chaff* over and over again for long periods. It is one of the first summer visitors to arrive in Britain each year.

The **tree sparrow** looks very much like the familiar house sparrow, but if you look at its head you will see it has a chestnut brown crown instead of the grey one of the other bird. Look for the tree sparrow in open woods, parks and large gardens. The stout beak shows that it is a seed-eater.

The **redstart** is a summer visitor to Europe. The female is less brightly coloured than the male, but both sexes have a red tail. Redstarts are insect-eaters and like to live in woods, parks and orchards with old trees. They make their nests in holes in trees, and sometimes in old walls.

The **nightingale** is famous for its beautiful song. It sings by day as well as by night, but you can hear it best at night for few other birds will be singing. A summer visitor to Europe, the nightingale likes thick woodland and is not easy to see. Its slender beak tells you that it eats insects.

The **crossbill** is another member of the finch family, and if you look at its beak you will see that it is well named. The tips of the beak cross over and are specially designed for opening the cones of spruce and other conifers to get at the seeds. Look for it in coniferous trees in woods and parks.

The **lesser spotted woodpecker** is the smallest of our woodpeckers, being no larger than a sparrow. The female has no red on her head. Look for the bird in deciduous woods, orchards and large gardens. It searches the tree trunks for insects and will even take seeds from the bird table.

The **crested tit** is easily recognised by its black and white crown and crest of feathers. It occurs in mixed woodlands in southern Europe, but elsewhere you must look for it among the conifers. In Britain it is found only in certain Scottish pine woods. It eats insects in summer and small seeds in winter.

The **willow tit** lives in all kinds of woodland and has no strong connection with willow trees, despite its name. It feeds mainly on insects and nests in holes . The marsh tit also lives in the woodlands. It is very similar to the willow tit but has a glossier black crown and a smaller black bib.

Long ears, thin wings

A quick glance at the drawing on the right should immediately give you a clue to the name of the creature pictured there. It is a long-eared bat and, at 30 mm long, its ears are not much shorter than its whole body!

The long-eared bat likes to live in areas with scattered trees so you can often find it flying about in town parks and village streets. But you will have to wait until after dark to see it because, like all our bats, it sleeps by day. You might be lucky enough to come across such a creature sleeping upside-down in a deep crevice in a tree or building. You might even find bats in the roof of your house! But remember never to disturb them. They don't do any harm and might actually do a lot of good by catching furniture beetles (page 27) and other insect pests. If you do find a bat's bedroom, try watching it carefully at sunset: you may see the bat come out and groom itself thoroughly before setting off on its night-time hunt.

The long-eared bat can usually be recognised at night by its slow, fluttering flight around the trees, for most other bats fly faster and higher. Notice how the bat's wings are formed from thin skin stretched between the animal's very long fingers and its back legs.

Moths are the favourite prey of this bat. It catches some while in flight but will also pluck its dinner from the leaves of trees and bushes. It even hovers in mid-air, as you can see in the picture, while scanning the plants with its "radar" to see if there is any food about. High-pitched sounds sent out through the bat's mouth bounce back to the large ears as echoes, and the bat can actually tell the difference between those bouncing back from leaves and those from moths.

In the winter there are few insects for these bats to eat. How do you think they survive through the cold weather?

Hunt the bat

It is always worth having a look in hollow trees for sleeping bats. They normally hang upside-down. Never disturb the animals if you find them. Here are three common kinds. Can you spot the differences?

Natterer's bat (below) lives in open country and light woodland and roosts in trees and buildings during the summer. It has a very long membrane, known as the tragus, in its ear.

The **pipistrelle** (below) sleeps in narrow crevices in trees and buildings. At under 45 mm long it is Europe's smallest bat.

The **noctule** (below) can be recognised by its rich red coat. It lives mainly in woodland and often roosts in large colonies.

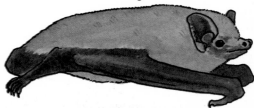

A prickly plant

If you've ever tried to gather holly to make Christmas decorations you will know that the leaves are extremely prickly. The spines are a good defence against humans of course, but their real job is to defend the holly against deer and other animals that might try to nibble its leaves.

Because these prickly leaves make such a good barrier, the holly has often been planted in hedgerows where it often grows quite tall. Have a look at one of these hedgerow holly trees. What do you notice about the leaves on the higher branches? Can you think why these upper leaves are not prickly?

The natural home of the holly is not the hedgerow but the deciduous forest, where it grows under the spreading branches of the oaks, beeches and other large trees. Not many plants can survive under the dense shade of the beech, but the holly manages to do so because it is an evergreen. Its tough leaves can make food in the winter when the beech has lost its leaves and the sunlight can get through to the lower levels. But the holly rarely gets very tall in the woods: most of the time it remains as just a prickly bush.

In the picture you can see the holly's bright red berries. But have you noticed that not all holly trees bear such fruits? This is because the male and female flowers grow on different trees and only female ones can produce the shiny red berries. See if you can spot the flowers on the trees in May. They are small and white, as you can see in the picture, and sweetly scented. The fruits turn red in time for Christmas and attract birds like the mistle thrush shown here. Use your *Nature Diary* to record what birds you see eating the fruits. They eat them much earlier in cold winters than in mild ones.

Quickthorn hawthorn

Look for hawthorn trees in the hedgerows. You won't have far to look because the hawthorn is our commonest hedgerow tree. You can recognise it by its deeply notched leaves and woody thorns. It has bunches of creamy flowers in May and deep red fruits, called haws, in the autumn. It is one of the best trees for hedges because it grows very quickly and its thorns make a good barrier. The rapid growth is responsible for the tree's alternative name of quickthorn.

Root your own hedge

The hawthorn is one tree that will grow very quickly from a cutting. You can see this for yourself by carrying out this simple project in spring.

1 Pull a slender twig from a branch so that it has a "heel" at the base.

2 Plant the cutting in a pot of sand and peat and put it in the garden. Keep it moist, but not too wet.

3 Gently remove the cutting from the pot after about 6 weeks. It will probably have grown roots.

Name that tree!

Unless you take your walks high in the hills, you will always see trees around you. It is not very difficult to learn the names of the commoner species. Look at their leaves between spring and autumn for these are always a good guide – and with evergreen trees you can, of course, use their leaves all year round to help you identify them. The shape, texture and amount of division or toothing around the edge of the leaf are all important. And the flowers and fruits or cones are also very useful for identification. Studying the bark pattern may give you further clues, and in winter you can often identify the deciduous trees by the shape and colour of their buds. With experience, you can even identify a tree just from its shape!

The leaves, flowers and fruits of some common trees are shown here. Those labelled D are deciduous trees while those labelled E are evergreen.

D

The **horse chestnut** is easily identified by its compound, fan-shaped leaves (see page 8), its beautiful flower spikes, its "conkers" and its sticky buds.

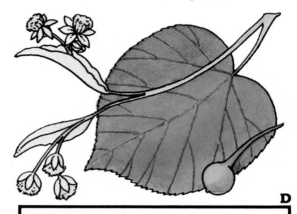

D

The **common lime** has rather rough, heart-shaped leaves. Each bunch of sweet-smelling flowers has a leafy "wing" which later carries the fruits away on the wind.

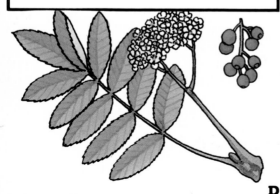

D

The **rowan**, also called the mountain ash, grows wild in the hills, but has been planted in many towns by man. The leaves each have 9-19 leaflets. Birds enjoy the orange fruits.

D

The **plane** is easily recognised by its flaky, mottled bark (see page 4) and by its little balls of flowers and fruits. The tree we see in parks and streets is the London plane.

The **aspen** is a poplar whose leaves tremble in the slightest breeze. Its flowers are carried in male or female catkins which grow on separate trees. You'll find it in damp places.

The **alder** grows in damp woods and on river banks. The male flowers are carried in catkins which open early in spring. The female flowers grow in small cone-like catkins.

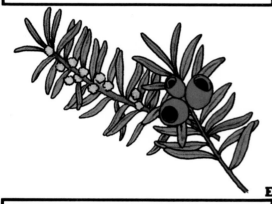

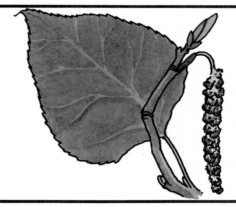

The **yew** has dark green leaves and is related to the pine. The male trees produce pollen held in tiny yellow cones. The seeds grow on female trees in fleshy pink cups.

The **Lombardy poplar** is a tall, slim tree which is often planted to form wind-breaks or to screen buildings. It has shiny leaves and, like all poplars, carries its flowers in catkins.

The **cedar of Lebanon** is a conifer with huge horizontal branches. It is planted as an ornamental tree in parks and large gardens. The cones fall to pieces when they are ripe.

Lawson cypress has scale-like leaves all over its twigs and a strong smell. The cones are small and round. The tree itself is usually conical, and much planted in gardens.

The farmer's friend

Look closely at the owl on the right. It is called a little owl and, like its bigger cousins, it is a perfect hunting machine. Look at the large eyes, specially designed to spot the slightest movement, and the powerful claws used to snatch and kill its prey. Notice, too, the sharp, hooked beak with which it tears the food to pieces.

At only 22 cms long, the little owl is one of the smallest European owls and, as you would expect, it catches fairly small animals for its food. Insects, including moths, earwigs and many beetles, make up more than half of its diet. And since many of these are pests of our farm and garden crops, the little owl is a friend of the farmer. It also catches mice and voles and some small birds – especially sparrows and young starlings.

Most owls hunt at night, but the little owl does a lot of its hunting in the daytime. Look for it in open country, perching on hedgerow trees and fence posts. It often uses these when scanning the surrounding countryside for food, and it may have several favourite perches scattered throughout its territory. If you are lucky enough to see a little owl and approach it, the bird will probably get rather agitated: watch how it bobs its head nervously up and down. If you get even closer it will take off for one of its other perches. Notice its rising and falling flight and listen out also for its call of *keeoo-keeoo* – sounding rather as if it is complaining about the disturbance.

If you can find one of the little owl's regular perches, try looking underneath it for owl pellets. These contain indigestible material which the owl has spat out. You might find the fur and bones of small mammals and the tough wing cases of beetles inside. The contents will give you a good guide to what the owl has been eating.

nature detective

Other owls

Look and listen for these other owls in the countryside. They usually hunt by night, but you can sometimes find them resting in the trees. The scops owl, under 20 cms long, lives in open country but not in Britain. Look for the tawny owl in trees in parks and open woodland. Listen for its hooting call at night. The long-eared owl lives mainly in woods. Its "ears" are really tufts of feathers. The barn owl flies around farms and villages. Its white feathers give it a ghost-like appearance.

Scops owl

Tawny owl

Long-eared owl

Barn owl

Under the bark

The insect in the circle is an elm bark beetle and, along with many others like it, it has been responsible for the death of millions of elm trees. This happens because many of the beetles carry Dutch elm disease, a fungus which blocks the water-carrying tubes of the elms. Starved of water, the branches gradually die and, eventually, so might the whole tree. The elm in the middle of the picture is dying: see how its leaves are turning yellow.

The female elm bark beetle chews her way into the elm tree in order to breed. She excavates a vertical tunnel or *gallery* just under the bark and then lays eggs at intervals along it. When the eggs hatch the grubs start to tunnel themselves, feeding on the rich tissues just under the bark. They always tunnel away from the main gallery and, as they grow, their tunnels get wider. You can see the intricate tunnel patterns on the right of the picture. Look for them on elm trunks and also on fallen bark.

When the beetle grubs are fully grown they turn into pupae and, finally, adult beetles. They will have already caused considerable damage to the tree through their tunnelling as grubs. But as they escape through the bark as adults they are capable of causing far more harm – by carrying Dutch elm disease with them to another tree. If the tree in which they hatched has the disease, then the escaping beetles will pick up some of the germs and spread them to new elms.

There are many other kinds of bark beetle, each making its own tunnel pattern in its own particular species of tree. Look for their galleries on ash and pine trunks, but don't ever pull the bark away from living trees to help you in your search – this will harm them even more.

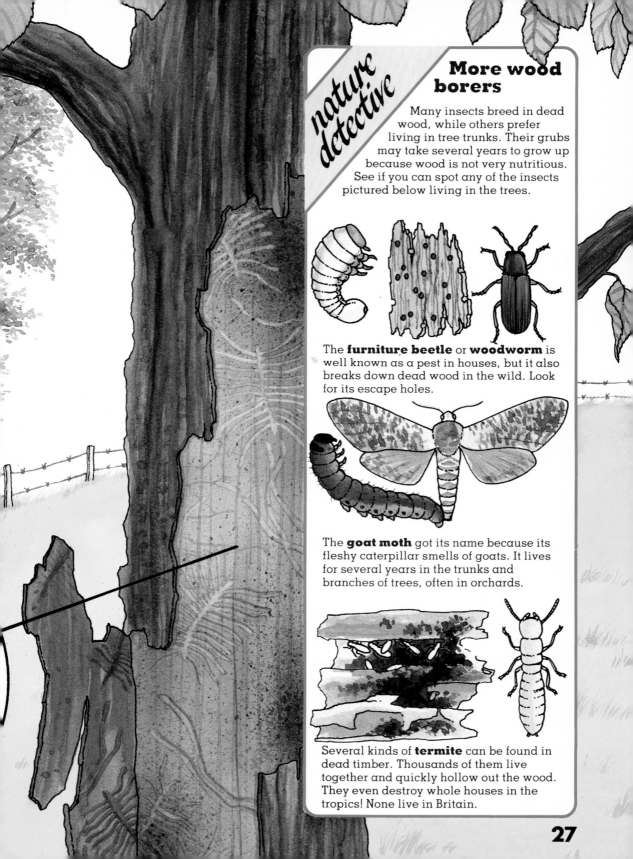

More wood borers

Many insects breed in dead wood, while others prefer living in tree trunks. Their grubs may take several years to grow up because wood is not very nutritious. See if you can spot any of the insects pictured below living in the trees.

The **furniture beetle** or **woodworm** is well known as a pest in houses, but it also breaks down dead wood in the wild. Look for its escape holes.

The **goat moth** got its name because its fleshy caterpillar smells of goats. It lives for several years in the trunks and branches of trees, often in orchards.

Several kinds of **termite** can be found in dead timber. Thousands of them live together and quickly hollow out the wood. They even destroy whole houses in the tropics! None live in Britain.

27

An elegant evergreen

The tree on the right is a Scots pine. It is our commonest conifer and you can easily identify it by the brick-red bark on the upper part of its trunk. A native of the mountains and cool northern regions, the pine has been planted in many other places to supply timber. What's more, its winged seeds can travel long distances on the breeze, so it has also sprung up on many sandy heaths and commons. In other words, you won't ever have to go far to find this elegant evergreen!

There are many different kinds of pine, but all bear their needle-like leaves in small bunches. The Scots pine carries its needles in pairs, like most other northern species. Feel the tough needles – they have to be hardy like this to withstand the winter winds. Examine the cones in spring. You will find the female cones growing in three different stages, as you can see in the picture. The little red cones at the tips of the twigs are the new female cones: you can think of them as flowers at this stage. They won't grow any more until they have received some pollen from the male cones. You will find the male cones further back on the twigs, forming dense yellow clusters. Tap the twigs and you'll see the clouds of pollen drifting from the cones. This pollinates the females which then start to swell and turn green as the seeds grow inside them. After one year they look like the green cone at the bottom of the picture, but it will be another year before they are woody and ripe enough to scatter their seeds.

Many cones never get to scatter their seeds at all because of the crossbill, which you can see on the right of the picture. This colourful bird uses its strange beak to open the cones and pull out the seeds before they can be scattered.

nature project

Adopt a tree

If you have a favourite tree, you might like to keep a diary about it. You can choose any kind of tree and it doesn't matter if it is evergreen or deciduous. It can be in the woods or in a park, or even in your garden. Visit your tree regularly – at least once a week – and note down everything that you see. If it is a deciduous tree, record the dates on which the buds open and also when you see the first flowers. When are the fruits ripe? When do the leaves change colour? When does the last leaf fall? Don't forget to include notes on all the animals that visit your tree as well. Write down every kind of animal that arrives and try to discover what it is. At the end of the year you will have a very interesting story to tell!

nature watch

Forecast the weather

If you look at fallen cones under the pines you will find them shut on damp days and open on dry ones. Take a cone home and hang it by your door: if it closes it means that the air is damp and rain might be on the way!

There is a good reason for the cone's movements. If it opened to drop its seeds in wet weather then the seeds would get wet and heavy and just fall to the ground under the tree.

By opening only when it is dry, the cone gives its seeds a better chance of drifting away on the wind and finding new places in which to grow.

Shelves of fungus

When you're next out walking, take a closer look at the trunks of some old deciduous trees. You'll probably find that on many of them there are large fungi sticking out from the trunks like shelves. You might come across many different kinds but they all belong to the same large group known as bracket fungi. The one on the right is known as the dryad's saddle. It got its name because people once imagined that dryads, which are legendary woodland fairies, sat astride the saddle-shaped fungi. Up to 60 cms across, the dryad's saddle is easily recognised by the rings of brown scales on its upper surface and also by the black stalk which joins the fungus to the tree. It grows mainly on elms, but also on sycamore and other large trees, and can be seen in spring and summer. Look at the undersides of the shelves and you will see that they are very spongy, and covered with thousands of small pores. When the fungus is ripe, millions of tiny spores fall from these pores and are blown away by the wind to grow into more bracket fungi.

The fungal shelves that you see are only a small part of the fungus – for inside the trunk are masses of hair-like threads, branching through the timber and taking food from it. They eventually cause the timber to rot and kill the tree, but the fungus goes on living, even on dead wood.

The dryad's saddle is quite a soft fungus and does not remain on the trees for very long. Flies and other insects lay their eggs on the shelves and their grubs tunnel through the soft flesh and eat it. The green woodpecker, which you can see in the picture, soon learns about the grubs and their hiding place and pecks away at the fungus to find its dinner. By autumn, there is not much left!

nature watch

On the bark

The bracket fungi actually feed from the trees on which they grow, but many other small plants merely perch on the trunks and branches without taking any food from their host. These perchers are called *epiphytes* and they are most common in damp places. You might even find that some trees in moist woodlands are completely clothed with them! Mosses and lichens are the most abundant of these epiphytes. The lichens are less green than the mosses and have no leaves: many of them form grey crusts on the trees, but others form dense tufts that hang from the trunks and branches like beards.

Name that bracket!

Look for bracket fungi on all kinds of deciduous tree trunks and dead stumps. Some kinds occur only on certain kinds of trees. Look for the dust-like spores under the brackets: the spore colour often helps to identify the species.

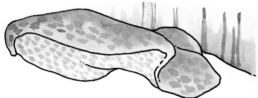

The **birch bracket** *(above)* has very tough, rubbery flesh. It grows on living and dead birch trunks and can be found throughout the year.

The **beefsteak fungus** *(above)* grows on oaks during the autumn. It has the colour and texture of raw beef.

The **jew's ear** *(above)* is not a real bracket fungus and has no spongy pores. Look for its ear-shaped growths on elder trees.

Coriolus versicolor *(above)* has no common name, but it's one of our commonest bracket fungi. Look for it on dead stumps and fallen timber. Feel its furry surface.

The **swan-necked thread moss** *(left)* grows mainly at the base of tree trunks. Notice the drooping spore capsules which give the plant its name.

Graphis elegans *(right)* is a lichen which forms grey crusts on tree trunks. The dark patches, looking like scribbles, are where the spores are produced.

Builders aloft

When spring arrives, one of the first birds to start building its nest is the noisy rook. Look for these large black birds carrying twigs among the tree tops as early as February. They build their nests in the tops of the tallest trees they can find and are not at all bothered by the wind, even when it threatens to dislodge their high-rise homes. The birds like beech, elm and other large deciduous trees, and their bulky nests are very easy to see among the bare branches. The nests are always built in colonies, called rookeries, and the birds use the same trees year after year. You'll find rookeries in groups of trees on farmland or by rivers, but you won't find them in the woods.

Use your binoculars to watch the rooks at work in the spring. The males snap off quite large twigs, which the females then weave cleverly into the nest. You might even see a male steal twigs from a neighbour's nest! Mud, grass, wool, roots and many other materials are used to line the nest and, once it's finished, the female lays up to nine eggs inside it. She will sit on them for about 20 days, while the male bird brings her food. The baby rooks leave the nest when they are about a month old, but they spend a few days hopping about in the branches before trying out their wings.

Although rooks always nest in the trees, they feed on the ground. Look for them roaming the fields in flocks as they search for worms and insects. They also eat grain and meat – in fact, you can often see them feasting on dead rabbits on the road.

Try to find out the differences between rooks and crows. One obvious difference is that the crow has no grey on its face.

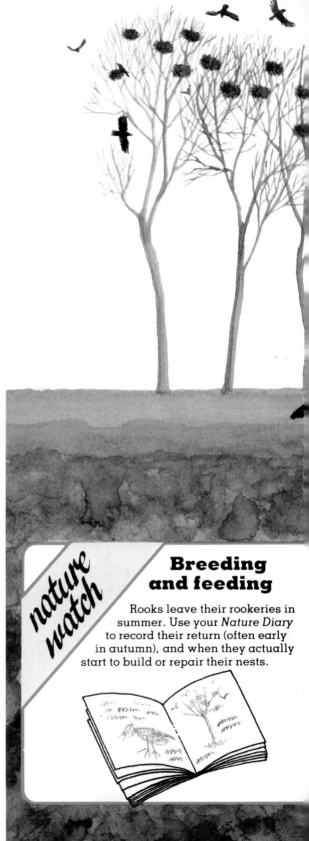

nature watch

Breeding and feeding

Rooks leave their rookeries in summer. Use your *Nature Diary* to record their return (often early in autumn), and when they actually start to build or repair their nests.

The rook's stout beak can deal with most kinds of food. The bird often digs it into the ground to capture cockchafer grubs which are one of its favourite foods – in fact these grubs are commonly known as rookworms! They are enemies of the farmer, so the rook is actually doing some good by eating them – even if it does take some grain as well.

If you explore the ground below a rookery, especially in autumn or spring, you will probably find numerous pellets like the one shown below. They contain mainly chaff from the grain that the birds have eaten. The chaff is indigestible and, together with small stones, it is coughed up and spat out as a pellet.

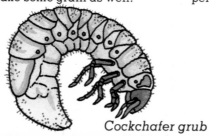

Cockchafer grub

Rook pellet

Hunter in the wilderness

Few people are ever lucky enough to see the beautiful pine marten outside a zoo. It is a rather shy animal and lives mainly in dense pine forests, so to see it living wild in the British Isles you will have to go to the wilder parts of the north and west. On the continent, however, the pine marten is more widely distributed and you can often find it living in deciduous forests as well as among the pines.

The pine marten is about the size of a cat, with a head and body varying from 40 to 50 cms in length. Its bushy tail is about another 20 cms long. Like the squirrel, the pine marten uses this long tail to help it steer and keep its balance when scampering through the branches. It is an incredibly agile animal in the trees, but actually spends more time on the ground than up in the branches. It is a very fast runner indeed!

If you are in pine marten country have a look for the animal's tracks in soft ground. You can see what they look like from the panel on the right. The individual footprints are 4-5 cms across and show five paw marks. The marten usually bounds along in great leaps, so its prints appear in groups of four with up to a metre between each group. The animal sometimes trots along,

however, and then its footprints are strung out in a line. Look also for the pine marten's droppings – a sure sign that the animal is about. Black or dark grey, the droppings are up to 10 cms long and usually twisted and drawn out into a long point at one end. They are usually deposited in a regular spot, often raised up on a tree stump or fallen log. And, unlike the droppings of the polecat and beech marten, those of the pine marten have a rather sweet scent!

Pine martens are fiercely carnivorous animals, feeding mainly on rodents and small birds. Most of their hunting is done on the ground, but they often chase and catch squirrels in the trees. The one in the picture is about to bound after the passing red squirrel. Notice the animal's beautiful thick fur. Pine martens are hunted for their fur in some northern regions.

nature detective

Spot the difference

The beech marten (below) does not live in Britain or in northern Europe, but it is quite common in southern and central Europe. It is quite similar to the pine marten, but can you see the one big difference? Beech martens, also known as stone martens, prefer deciduous woodlands to the coniferous forests and also enjoy life on rocky hillsides. They are quite common on farmland, often making their dens in barns and other outbuildings. This doesn't worry the farmer, though, since they are quite useful creatures to have around – catching a lot of mice as well as numerous sparrows.

The drawings above show the footprints of a running marten, with the prints strung out in a fairly straight line. The prints of the pine marten and beech marten are almost identical, although those of the beech marten are slightly smaller. Pine marten prints also tend to be rather blurred because the pine marten's feet are somewhat hairier than those of the beech marten.

Measuring trees

If you adopt a tree, as suggested on page 29, you will certainly want to know how tall it is. You will probably want to know how old it is as well. On this page you can find out how to discover both the height and the age of a tree by making some simple measurements. You can also find out how to make simple pictures of the leaves and bark to help you build up a complete record of your chosen tree.

How high is that tree?

There are several methods for estimating the height of trees, and two very simple ones are described here.

Method 1: For the first method you will need a ruler or a straight stick and a friend to help you. Ask your friend to stand at the base of the tree while you walk away from it. When you are some distance apart, hold the ruler or stick upright at arm's length in front of you and walk backwards or forwards until the bottom of the ruler is lined up with the bottom ot the tree and the top of the ruler coincides with the top of the tree. Remain at that point and turn the ruler until it is horizontal, still keeping it at arm's length. Align one end with the base of the tree and then ask your friend to walk away from the tree at right angles to your own direction. When your friend appears to be at the other end of the ruler you must shout stop. The distance between your friend and the tree itself will be the same as the height of the tree. Pace out the distance, and, by measuring the length of your stride, you can calculate the height of the tree.

Method 2: For the second method you need only a straight stick cut to the same length as the distance from your eye to your outstretched hand. Hold the stick upright in front of you and move backwards or forwards until the stick is lined up with the top and bottom of the tree, exactly as in the first method. At this point, because your arm and the stick are the same length, the distance from you to the tree must be the same as the height of the tree (this is a mathematical law). Pace out the distance to the tree and you will then know how high it is.

You might like to test the accuracy of each method by measuring something of known height, like a church tower. When you have measured a number of trees, you'll be able to guess at tree heights fairly accurately.

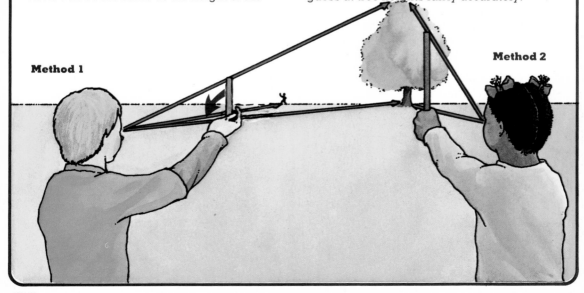

Method 1

Method 2

How old is that tree?

Have you ever looked at a freshly-cut tree stump or a felled trunk? If so, you will have seen a pattern of rings similar to those shown in the picture below. They are called *annual rings*. And each year, as the trunk gets thicker, another ring of wood is added just under the bark. This provides an excellent way of telling the age of a tree, since all you have to do is count the rings.

But what about a living tree? You can't cut it down just to find its age and, luckily, you don't have to! It has been discovered that most deciduous trees grow fatter at a similar rate, so simply by measuring a tree's girth or circumference at about 1.5 metres above the ground, you can get a good idea of its age. For mature trees growing by themselves – in a park, for example – the figure is 2.5 cms (one inch) of girth for every year of age. So a tree about 250 cms (100 inches) round would be about 100 years old. Woodland trees grow more slowly and would take about 200 years to reach this size. The method cannot be used for many conifers.

Leaf and bark rubbing

When making a study of a tree it is a good idea to record the shape of its leaves and also any bark pattern it may have. Rubbing is an easy way to do this. To make leaf rubbings, all you have to do is pick some fresh leaves and lay them on a flat surface. Cover them with a sheet of plain paper and then rub a soft pencil or crayon evenly all over the paper on top of each leaf, making sure you go right over the edges. The outline of each leaf and the pattern of its veins will then show up clearly on your paper.

Bark rubbing is a bit more difficult. You need a large piece of paper, and it is a good idea to tie it securely to your chosen trunk. Use a large wax crayon and rub it over a large area of the paper to pick up the bark pattern. Make sure, though, that the paper does not move whilst you're doing this. Then label the sheet with the name of the tree and keep it for future reference. Do all trees have similar bark patterns? Which tree has the smoothest bark? Keep your eyes open for small insects in the bark crevices as you work.

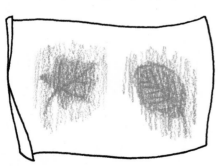

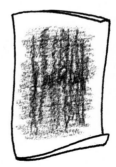

Pesky pigeons

The bird in the big picture is a wood-pigeon. Like the grey squirrel on page 6, you will find it almost wherever there are trees – in town parks and gardens, as well as in the woods. Listen for its soft song of cu-coo-coo-cu-cu as you walk through the woods. If you disturb the bird it will take off with a noisy flapping of wings and fly rapidly away. Look for the white bars on its wings as it flies.

The woodpigeon is about 40 cms long and is our largest pigeon. Like its relatives in the panel, it is almost entirely vegetarian. Watch out for it roaming the fields and parklands in huge flocks during the winter, feeding on cereals and other grasses, clovers and various other plants. The pigeons' liking for cabbages and other similar crops results in a great deal of damage so they are among the farmers' worst enemies.

If you watch the pigeons feeding in the fields during the year you may notice that there seem to be a lot more of them about during the winter. This is because our resident woodpigeon population is greatly increased at this time of year by birds flying in from the northern regions. As spring approaches the flocks tend to break up and the birds drift back to the woods, although you can see small flocks in the fields at any time of year. In the woods, the pigeons feed on tree buds and flowers and, later on, eagerly gobble up their fruits. Acorns and beech nuts are among their favourite woodland foods, but grain is the most important part of their diet in late summer and autumn.

Baby pigeons are reared in rather flimsy nests made of twigs and fed with a kind of milk from the parent's throat for the first few days of their lives, but they quickly move on to cereal grains and other seeds.

Town and country doves

Look for these relatives of the woodpigeon. You can see them in the town as well as in the country. They might look alike at first, but they are not difficult to distinguish if you look carefully. Try to listen to their calls as well.

The **town pigeon** (*above*) exists in many forms. It is a descendant of the wild rock dove which lives on cliffs, so it's quite at home living on buildings instead of in trees!

The **collared dove** (*right*) has a distinct black collar and black wing-tips. It feeds on grain. Its song is *coo-coooo-cu*, repeated over and over again.

The **stock dove** (*left*) is a little smaller than the woodpigeon and has no white patches. It is found mainly in woodland.

The end of a tree

A tree may live for 200 years or even more. In fact, some trees are known to be more than 2,000 years old! But, sooner or later, like every living thing, a tree must die. Its death might be hastened by fungi which will weaken the tree by invading any wounds made in its trunk. Wood-boring beetles and other insects can also easily get into the weakened timber and help to break it down still further.

Then along come certain birds, like the woodpecker, to peck holes in the trunk in their search for tasty insects. Eventually, after providing a home for hundreds of different plants and animals, the tree falls to the ground and begins to decay.

If you know of a fallen tree in your local woods, try to look at it regularly. Describe your discoveries in your *Nature Diary*. If you can visit it every month for a year or two you will see some great changes taking place. The trunk in the picture below is that of a beech tree, and on it you can see some of the fascinating plants and animals that still rely on the tree for food and shelter.

Fungi of many types soon colonise the decaying trunk. The big toadstools to the left of the picture are called ***Pholiota aurivella* (1)**. They grow on both living and dead beech

trunks and take away much of their goodness. **Trooping crumble-caps (2)** appear in their thousands in the autumn, especially in the later years of decay, while **candle snuff fungus (3)** is common throughout the year. **Tawny grisettes (4)** do not actually grow on the decaying wood, but commonly spring up around it.

As the bark decays and lifts away from the wood, many small animals make their homes underneath it. The **woodlouse (5)** and the **millipede (6)** feed on the decaying material, while the brightly coloured beetle known as *Endomychus coccineus* **(7)** feeds on the fungal threads that it finds growing there. The very flat larva of the **cardinal beetle (8)** spends its time feeding on various other insect grubs that it hunts for under the bark, while the male **stag beetle (9)** waits for a mate who will lay her eggs on the rotting timber. Of course, the presence of these insects means that many birds, like the **great spotted woodpecker (10)** still visit the trunk in their search for food.

All these plants and insects take many years to decompose a large trunk, but eventually it will disappear. Much of the food that was in it will return to the soil to nourish new plants. In fact, you can see the new **beech seedlings (11)** sprouting up around the trunk. One of these will eventually grow up to replace its dead predecessor and so provide a new home for a whole new set of creatures.

Picture index

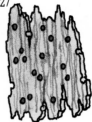
Panel index